CW01649899

THE THOUGHTS FROM ALAN'S PEN

ALAN PENN

The Thoughts From Alan's Pen

tellwell

Tellwell Talent
www.tellwell.ca

ISBN
978-0-2288-3632-2 (Hardcover)
978-0-2288-3631-5 (Paperback)
978-0-2288-3633-9 (eBook)

Table of Contents

Dedications

To my late parents,
Joy and Fred Penn, who taught
me right from wrong,
and whose example shaped me
into the person I am today.

To my sisters, Maureen and Adele, and twin sister Jackie,
thanks for your love and support.
To my Uncle Max and Auntie Sandra, Auntie Jocelyn
and Uncle Geffy, my nephews and nieces
and great nephews and great nieces and cousins...
I am nothing without my family.

To my cousin, Sandy Morris,
thanks for always being there for me,
through the good times and the bad.

To my special friends,
Ken, Nick, Josh, Ian, Dom, Flavio,
Hart, Daryl, Jeff, Ron,
Joe, Richard, and Michael,
thanks for being the brothers I never had.

To Mel and Gill,
thanks for treating me like family.

To Jack, Corinne, Rosanna,
Amy, Marcie, John D, Danielle, Luigi,
Glenn, Mike, John and Kevin,
thanks for your valued friendship.
And to those too many to mention
but equally as important...
I appreciate you all.
YouMeanALot
Alan

Acknowledgements

To my amazing illustrators...

David Medhurst (Toronto)

José Manuel Avendaño (Venezuela) chemapsuv@gmail.com

Praveen Singh (India) praveenkhati068@gmail.com

To my publishers...

The magnificent Tellwell self publishing team from Canada, especially Jennifer Chapin and Grace Gange and the designers. Thanks for making my dream come true!

'Teamwork made the dream work!'

A Note from the Author

I discovered I had a talent for writing poetry in 1993, when I was hospitalised for a nervous breakdown. I had an urge, a prompting, to write down how I felt, while I was depressed.

There was a famous poet, the late Dorothy Smith, from Hamilton, Ontario, also in my ward.

I introduced myself to her and showed her my poem. (It is featured in this book and was written as I was going through the different stages of depression.) She named it 'An Expression of Depression'.

She told me that she wrote haiku poetry. In fact, I found out later, she was a local radio personality from Hamilton, Ontario, Canada, and an award winning haiku poet. I had never heard of haiku. She explained what it was...three lines with a 5/7/5 syllable count. She invited me to write one for her, so I wrote:

> In the dentist's chair,
> waiting for my tooth and cash
> to be extracted.

When I showed it to her, she laughed loudly. That encouragement made me want to write another haiku poem for her. This then led to me writing many more. I had a notepad at my bedside, and I would write all the ideas that came to me, one after the other. My head was buzzing. I couldn't sleep. Many of the poems in this book were written during my hospitalisation. This new activity lifted me out of my depression.

Over the years, I kept writing and started to dream about having my poems and quotes illustrated and published in a book.

I wanted to create a book of poetry that would reflect everyday life, for the regular person to understand and enjoy.

I wasn't sure if my work was good enough, but after a lot of encouragement from those I shared my poems with, I knew I had a gift.

I kept procrastinating until after I recovered from cancer in 2016.

I knew I had to act quickly to create my legacy. Once that decision was made, everything came together.

I hope you enjoy what you read, that it will give you pause to think, give you a smile, make you laugh at yourself, and help you to appreciate life a little bit more.

YouMeanALot

Alan Penn

Foreword

Alan Penn has been quite a friend over the years. I'm impressed with this piece of work as it has taken him over twenty five years to bring this project to fruition. But now it is here, this splendid bit of artistry.

The brilliance behind a body of work like Alan's is unlike anything I've read in a long time.

I confess I am not normally a poetry reader; however, I enjoyed this immensely. The everyday situations and their common themes will help people deal with and relate to Alan's message.

I've known Alan for quite some time now, well over two decades, and in all that time the man has shown a creative side unrivalled by a life thwarted by obstacles. Everyone has a story, something they've lived through, endured and faced. Most of us stand and move forward as the wind of trouble buffets our face and chest. Others crumble under the weight of loss, strife and stress.

Alan has a different angle: he becomes creative. He adds wit and brilliance to life's unfairness, to life's beguilement. Like most people, Alan has faced a multitude of challenges in his life. His are more than the average person, suicide attempts, severe clinical depression (for which he was hospitalized four times), Crohn's disease, a rare form of multiple myeloma, two bankruptcies, divorce, and the loss of loved ones and close friends way too soon. Yet the man has battled through it all, by moving forward and creating.

The work found in this book will inspire those feeling uninspired, will lift the spirits of those dealing with depression, and will place a smile on the faces of those needing a boost to their spirit. In short, every reader will find something within the pages of this work to lighten their load, to bind tightly to, and to ease the chains mortality uses.

This book reminds us to be alive in the moment, to live a free existence, and to cherish with gratitude what we have, which is our health, our family, and our ability to choose a better way.

Join me now and take in each poem, each piece of literature, with a receptive mind and an overall feeling of openness. It's one thing to read something; it's something quite different to embrace, feel and experience it.

Alan, my dear friend, stay true and stay strong. Never stop and thank you for always being there.

Your friend,
Jonas Saul.
Author of the Sarah Roberts series

THAT'S LIFE

A Debt to Yourself

Once you have a credit card,
it soon becomes a get it card,
and turns into a sweat it card,
a never should have let it card.
So, make it a forget it card,
before it's a regret it card!

David Medhurst

'In a Cell' Phone

The cell phone, a revolution,
supposed to be a solution,
to connecting us all together.
But the opposite effect,
communication wrecked.
Who would have ever?

One to one chat and the internet,
videos, photos, music, and yet,
now we forget,
how to connect,
how to be polite,
and live life right.

In the subway, relax,
headphones at max.
Noise pollution,
a revolution?
Or playing a game,
so addictive, insane.

SONY
SAMSUNG
htc
David Medhurst

In a restaurant, out on a date,
phone rings, texts can't wait.
Manners rotten,
guest forgotten.
Pretty irate.

In the elevator,
stare at the screen,
twenty floors to go,
you'll never know,
what could have been.

Walking on the street,
crossing the road,
car horns blare,
without a care.
Flattened like a toad.

The 'in a cell' phone,
immobilising,
against socialising.
Immunisation,
against communication.
A revolution?

Jose Manuel Avendano

The Cigarette Addict

Here I am, dying for a smoke,
standing with all the other folk,
talking some gossip and sharing a joke,
having a drag and sipping a Coke.

David Medhurst

I speak and my voice starts to croak,
sounding like part girl, part bloke.
Even though they make me broke,
how I love my cough and choke!

David Medhurst

An Infection Reflection

In 2020, our lives were changed;
the year we all became estranged.
The year normal and fear exchanged.
How deranged!
Was it prearranged?

Grabbing for the good old days,
so fast they drifted far away,
don't leave us all, please stay,
don't leave our lives this way.
I beg You as I pray...

To You this message I send...
Let this insanity end.
In abnormality we descend,
driving us around the bend.
Will life ever mend?

Making most live in fear,
in this and every other year,
one thing is very clear,
the programming, so severe,
all common sense no longer here.

The elderly left hung to dry;
they've been written off to die.
On their own, they wondered, why?
Makes you want to cry.
What a way to say goodbye.

Praveen Singh Khati

No more cash.
Isn't that rash?
Not accepted in a flash.
That's OK, no backlash.
Our control sent to the trash.

Take a tape measure where you go,
'two metres apart' 'cause they told us so,
making it harder to say hello.
Talking through masks, communication slow.
The new normal? We don't know?

For twenty nine seconds wash your hands.
No supporters in the stands.
Vacation abroad...forget your plans.
No more hugs or shaking hands.
Our kids confused, don't understand.

They were warned this would happen...
governments got caught napping.
No one should be clapping.
The frontline's sapping.
Our economy's snapping.

We have to all shout out and yell
against this manufactured hell.
Let your numbers swell.
To your governments, rebel.
'We won't be kept in your cell!

We have one life to survive;
Don't live in fear; don't deprive.
Normal life we must revive,
if we want to succeed and thrive
or you'll die, though you're still alive.

Jose Manuel Avendano

Whether Forecast

Does it really matter whether
it's good or bad weather?

Weather that's cold,
weather that's hot,
whether it's raining,
whether it's not?

Jose Manuel Avendano

Weather that's windy,
weather that's humid,
whether it's great,
whether it's stupid?

Weather that thunders,
weather that snows,
whether it's foggy,
whether wind blows?

Jose Manuel Avendano

What matters is whether
you can BREATHE the weather.
If you can't FEEL the weather...
would the weather really matter?
And would it really matter whether??

Jose Manuel Avendano

The 'BIG C'

(dedicated to all those with or cured of cancer)

The BIG C, you're called
to make us quake,
shattering lives in your wake.

BIG C, big coward, you'll always be;
cowards are just BIG ZEROS, to me.

For when you're attacked, you run a mile.
BIG C, meet FU...enjoy your exile.

BIG C, one thing I know for sure...
in future, BIG C will mean BIG CURE!!

David Medhurst

Release Me from My Fat Cell

OK, that's it,
you have to leave!
My fat cell squatters...
you got the heave!

Today would be great,
but to be realistic,
that's not going to happen,
so don't go ballistic!

About thirty days,
that's all you've got,
brace yourselves,
for getting hot!

Jose Manuel Avendano

I'll be walking each day
for an hour,
sweating profusely,
then enjoying a hot shower.

Then off to the gym,
you're going to burn,
hotter than hell,
not my concern!

For the sooner you leave,
the less you'll suffer.
Don't even think
that I'm a bluffer!

Find another body
where you can squat for free.
My door is now closed...
I've thrown away the key.

Jose Manuel Avendano

No burgers, no beer and no more bread,
just chicken and veggies and shakes instead.
No candies, no cookies, no chocolate cake,
no gelato, no chips, no food that's fake.
No pasta, no pizza, no cheesecake, your fave,
no more of the good stuff I know that you crave!
No microwave meals to give you a snack;
no road to my heart for you to attack.
Flooding you with water to achieve my goal
of flushing you down the toilet bowl!!

Jose Manuel Avendano

Your luxuries, no longer provided,
get lost, fat cells,
for I've finally decided:

You're going to...

MELT, MELT, MELT,
so I can loosen my pants.
MELT, MELT, MELT,
I'm so happy I can dance.
MELT, MELT, MELT,
now it's on to romance!

Jose Manuel Avendano

Time of Your Life

Your clock of life ticks on,
never making a sound,
no need for batteries,
no need to be wound.

So, treasure every second
and do everything you've dared,
for when your clock stops...
it can never be repaired.

David Medhurst

PONDER THIS

Truth Sleuth

MIRROR, MIRROR, ON THE WALL,
NOTHING'S HIDDEN, YOU SEE IT ALL.

The sadness, the tears,
the madness, the fears.
The joy, the delight,
a happiness sight!

MIRROR, MIRROR, ON THE WALL,
NOTHING'S SECRET, YOU KNOW IT ALL.

The disappointments, the pain,
regrets that remain.
Excitement, celebration,
joy, jubilation.

MIRROR, MIRROR, ON THE WALL,
NOTHING'S FAKE, YOU FEEL IT ALL.

The truth, the confessions,
the reality, the lessons.
Dreams that come true,
loving what you do.

MIRROR, MIRROR, ON THE WALL,
NEVER FOOLED, YOU REVEAL IT ALL.

David Medhurst

The Most Powerful Thing in Life

More powerful than a nuclear bomb,
more powerful than a quake,
more powerful than a tsunami,
and the many lives it takes.

More powerful than a hurricane,
more powerful than an eruption,
more powerful than a famine,
or political corruption.

It's something you can't touch,
it's something you can't feel,
it's something you can't wear,
it's something you can't steal.

All we see and have,
was created by this power,
it's something we experience,
every second of every hour.

Hurry up and tell me,
you're making me distraught!
It's something we all have,
that something is a ...

THOUGHT !!!

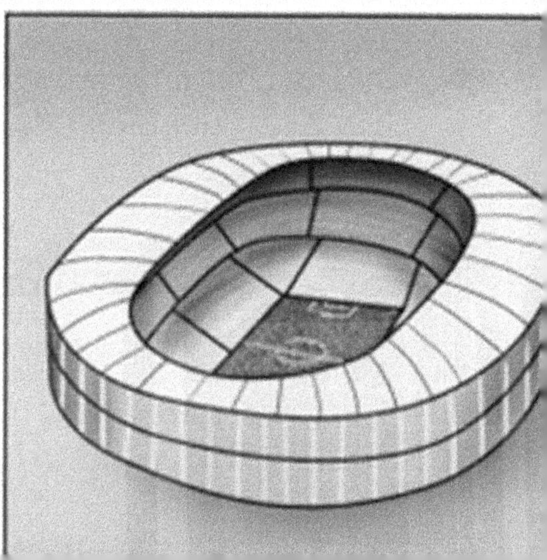

Jose Manuel Avendano

Thank Bank

Every night before you sleep, say,
Thank You for a pain free day.

Thank You my hands don't shake,
I'm in no pain or have pills to take.

Thank You for the gift of sight,
all these visions of delight.

Thank You I can laugh and weep,
I have no stress, to disturb my sleep.

Thank You for the gift of hearing,
the laughter, the joy and all the cheering.

Thank You for sounds that feed my spirit,
enriching my life and everything in it.

Jose Manuel Avendano

Thank You for the gift of speech,
that I can communicate and teach.

Thank You for the gift of taste,
to delight my senses and my waist.

Thank You for the gift of smell,
food, flowers, what surrounds me as well.

Thank You that I can use each hand,
I can feel, touch and grip on demand.

Thank You that I'm able to stand,
I can walk, cycle and run on command.

Jose Manuel Avendano

Thank You for my pets;
they make my heart swell.

Thank You for my memory
and the stories that I tell.

Thank You for my future,
my present and my past.

Thank You for each moment
and all that I've amassed.

Thank You for my home;
Thank You for my bed.

Thank You for my clothes
and that I'm always fed.

Thank You for the freedom
to be able to create.

Thank You for my Country,
where I'm free to choose my fate.

Jose Manuel Avendano

Thank You for each breath,
Thank You for my health.

Thank You for both,
for without I have no wealth.

Thank You for my family,
Thank You for each friend.

Thank You for each blessing
that You decide to send.

Thank You for my spirit
that makes me very humble.

Thank You for my willingness
to learn when I stumble.

Thank You for the lesson
I will never ignore...

that whenever you thank more...
you will always bank more.

David Medhurst

Words of Mass Destruction

We all own a lethal 'weapon'
that isn't made of steel,
ready to be fired,
depending how we feel.

Our mind is the commander,
and when it says, ATTACK!
we launch it from our mouths
and can never take it back.

The weapon is our temper,
our words, the ammunition,
poison tipped with venom,
to complete the demolition.

Jose Manuel Avendano

When it hits its target,
it cannot be removed,
the wounds cannot be stitched
and can never be improved.

First attacking confidence,
extinguishing the spirit,
destroying the person's soul
and everything that's in it.

Next comes an explosion,
boom goes self esteem,
and the fuel the spirit needs
to power every dream.

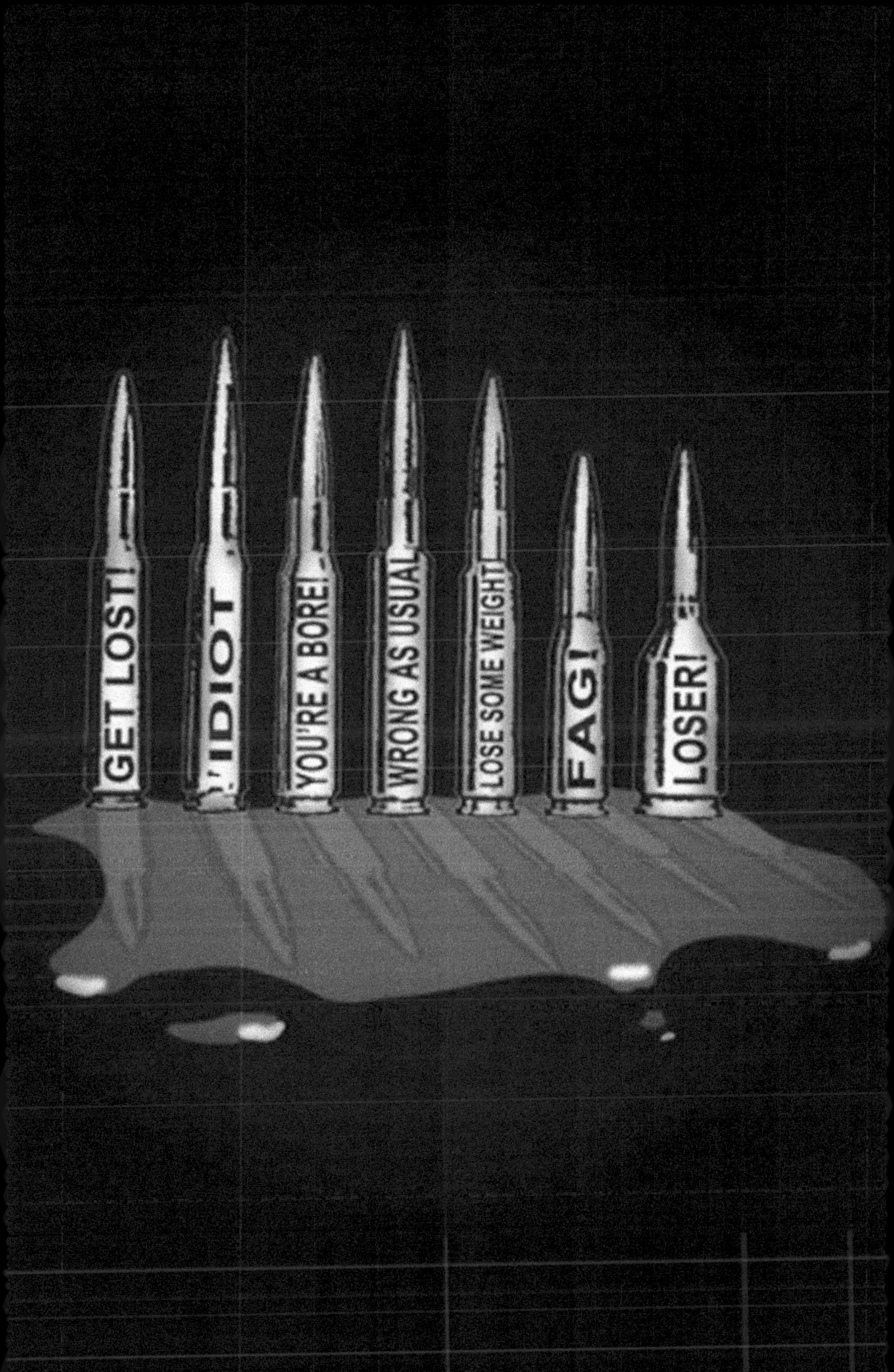

David Medhurst

So next time you get the urge,
and are feeling the desire,
to load up your 'weapon'
pull the trigger and fire...

Think for a few seconds,
about delaying your attack,
realise when you launch your words,
they aren't coming back.

Throw away your anger
and your 'weapon' too,
only 'kill' with kindness;
make your words heal them and you.

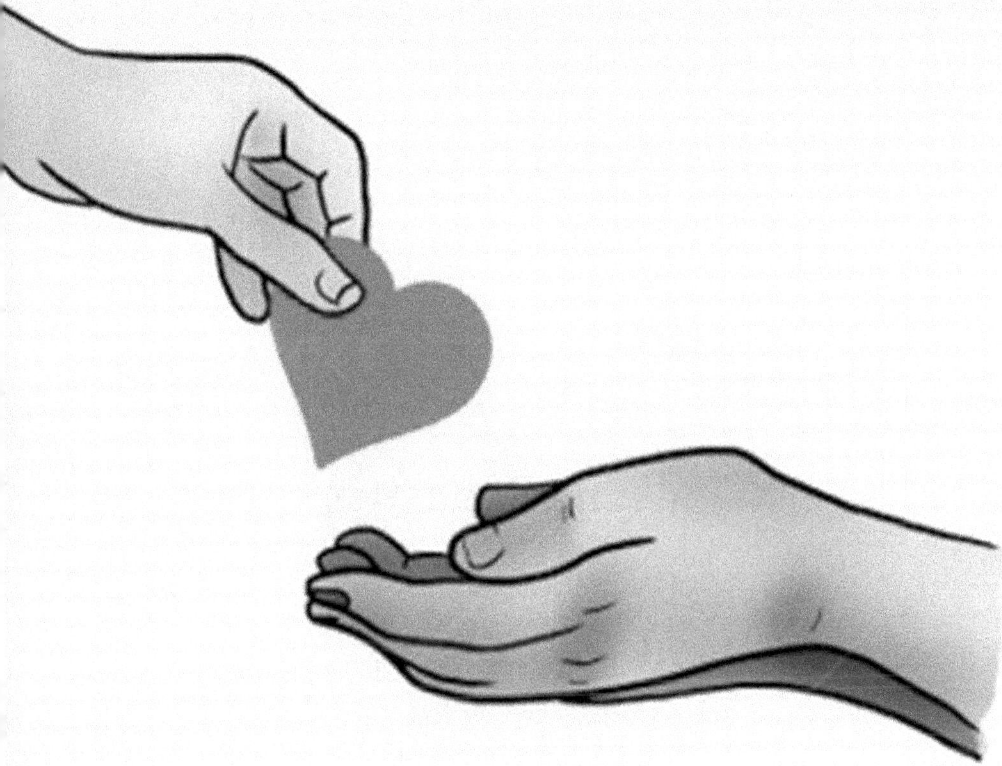

Jose Manuel Avendano

The Hate Dynasties

Racists aren't born,
they are people who are taught;
their 'teachers' commit this crime...
without ever being caught!

David Medhurst

A War Worth Fighting For

The fight against racism
has only just begun;
for future generations,
this battle must be won.

In order to succeed
we can no longer ignore,
this bitter tasting apple
that's rotten to the core.

People who are prejudiced
can't see anything wrong,
telling those who'll listen...
"Minorities don't belong!"

But the bigots don't object
when our Country's called to fight,
then there's no such problem,
they're now equal overnight.

Praveen Singh Khati

If you needed a blood transfusion
as you lay dying in your bed,
would you see the different colours
mixed in with the red?

If the answer to that is 'no',
then doesn't that prove my case?
Everyone's the same...
we're all one human race.

So, racists hear my words
and give yourselves a shake;
be an example for your children,
teach them right for goodness sake!

Help end all this hatred
and unnecessary grief;
accept one whose skin colour differs
or who follows another belief.

Please don't turn your backs now
and put all the wrongs to right;
give us a world without hatred,
a world you can help to unite!

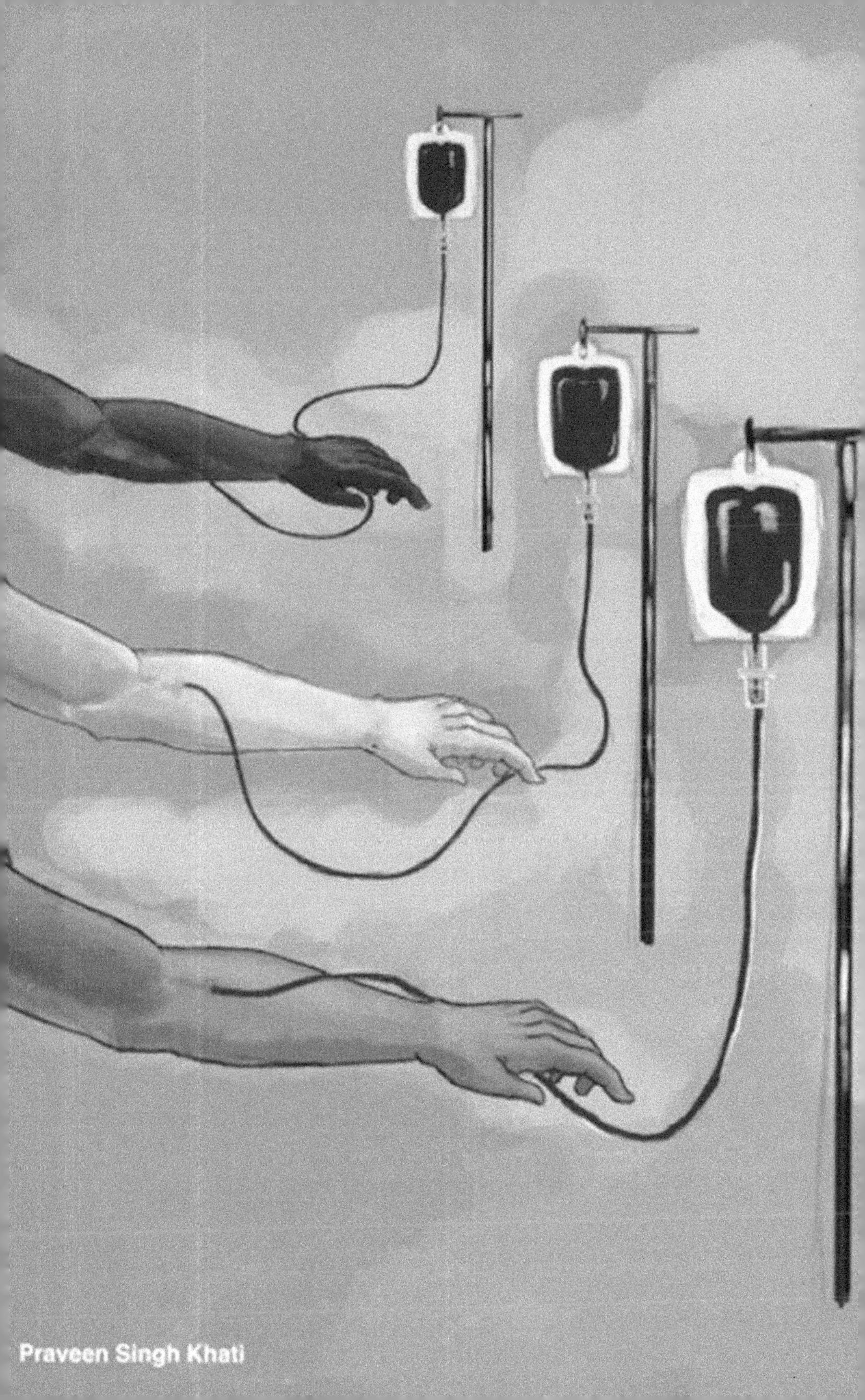
Praveen Singh Khati

An Unhealthy Diet

A book can make you wealthy,
but like a stomach that's never fed,
the 'food' between its covers,
will starve you if not read.

David Medhurst

An Amazing World

Isn't it amazing
how telescopes see the stars,
and space probes have been sent
to Jupiter and Mars?

Isn't it amazing,
our world a click away,
emails and texting
send instantly what we say?

Isn't it amazing,
with a few strokes of a knife,
a surgeon can transplant a heart
and save a human life?

Jose Manuel Avendano

Isn't it amazing,
although winter comes each year,
that accidents are so many,
as motorists drive in fear?

Isn't it amazing
that cities grind to a halt,
for if it snows in this modern world,
all they can use is...SALT!!

Praveen Singh Khati

The Delusion

We think that money makes us rich
and fulfils our every need;
just remember if you're poor...
you can be very rich in deed.

David Medhurst

Voices

Those voices inside your head
will be with you "til you're dead,
saying that you can't...instead,
tell them while you're lying in bed,
you're no longer going to dread,
the bad things always said,
stopping you going ahead.

Hush now voices that tread,
through the pathways of your head.
Your taunts no longer fed
until bad thoughts will have fled.
Only good things to be said,
spirit eager to be led.

Fuel your dreams and move ahead
to live a life not misled
by those voices inside your head.
So that when you're dead,
your LEGACY...widespread.

David Medhurst

The Storm of Life

(dedicated to Phoinyx Wittingham)

As you travel along life's rocky road
and a storm looms up ahead...
be prepared to face it,
don't run away in dread.

For as the lightning flashes,
it lights up the road below,
and guides you on your journey,
by showing you where to go.

David Medhurst
STORM
OF LIFE
AHEAD

When you battle through your problems,
not knowing what to do,
be thankful for the howling winds,
and they will push you through.

Get excited about the bad times;
good times are around the bend,
just keep on battling until it hurts,
just keep on until the end.

And when you finally make it,
the storm will celebrate too,
for the lightning will be dancing,
and the thunder clapping you!!

Jose Manuel Avendano

PENNISMS

Toxic

People who are toxic

talk sick!

Avoid them!

David Medhurst

NO ENTRY

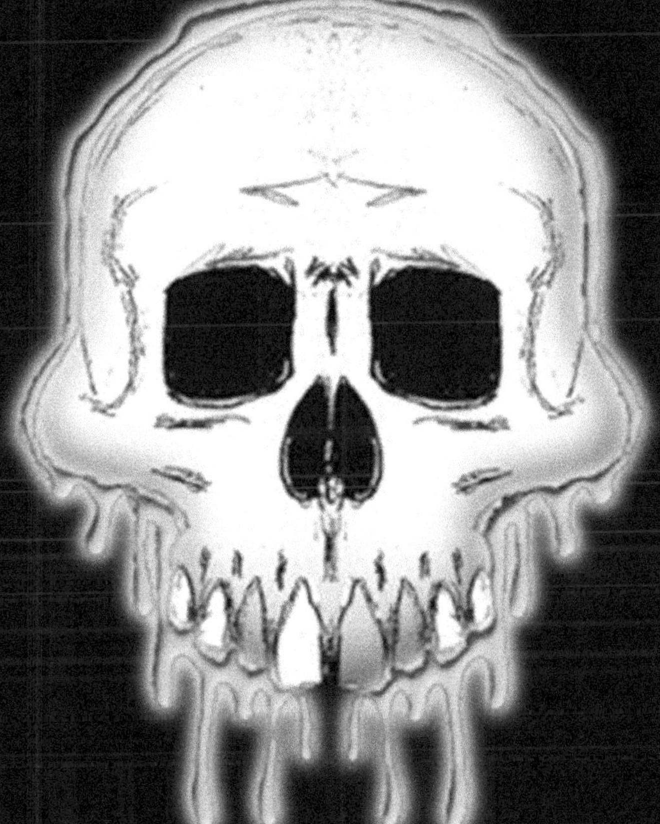

TOXIC PEOPLE

Passionate

(dedicated to my brother
Hart Hayden)

When you're passionate,
don't ration it.

Jose Manuel Avendano

Appreciation

Appreciation feeds the soul.

avid Medhurst

Advice

Take my advice...

take your hand

off your vice!

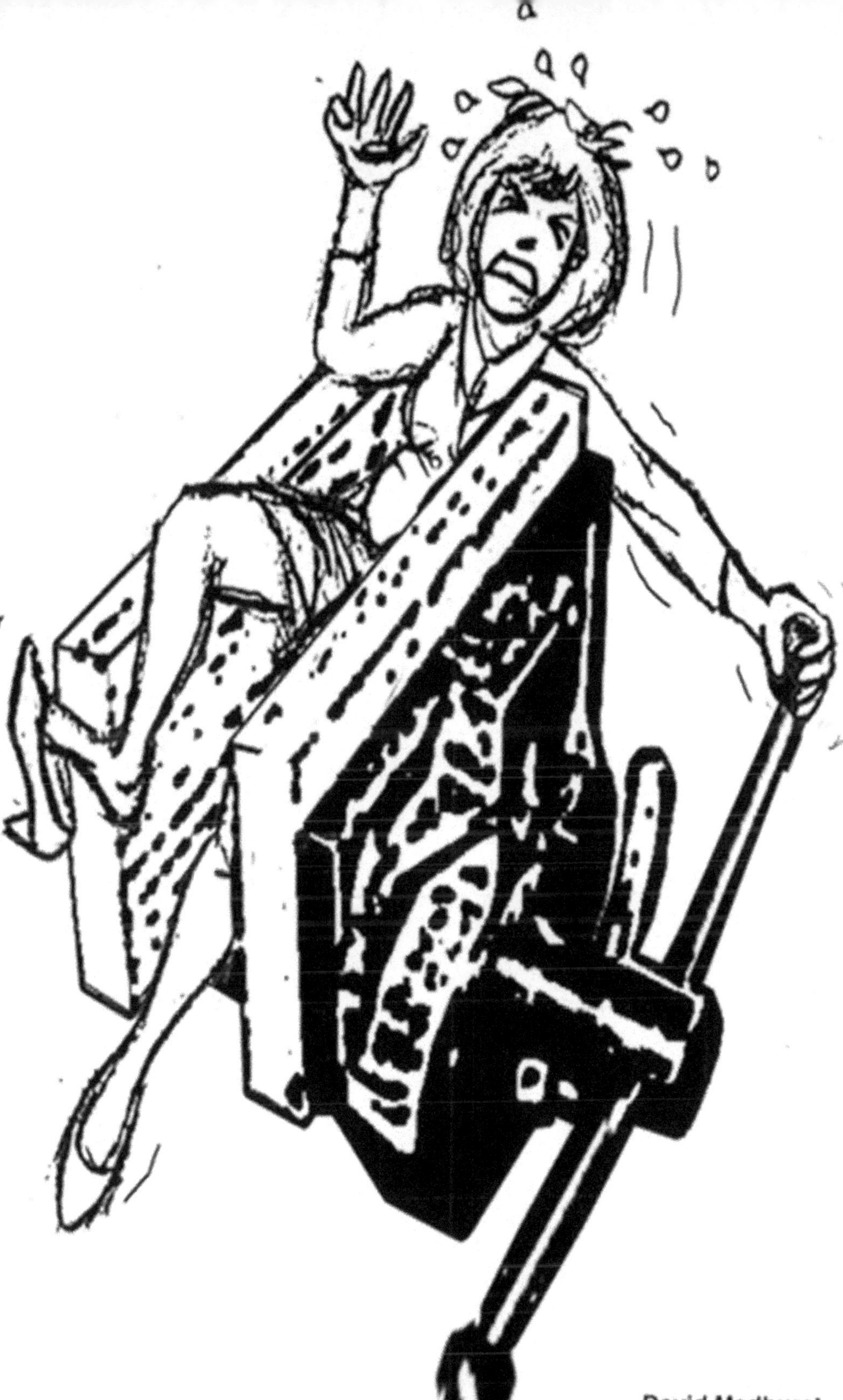

David Madhurst

AN EXPRESSION OF DEPRESSION

Part 1

The Depression

Sitting alone in a darkened room,
accompanied by thoughts of doom and gloom,
frightened, confused, full of self doubt,
trapped in a cage with no way out!

The characters in this poem are different at each stage, to indicate how many different types of people from all walks of life, are affected by this disease.

David Medhurst

Feeling hungry, not wanting to eat,
the telephone rings, you stay in your seat.
Answering the phone's too much of a strain,
talking to people, too much of a pain.

Jose Manuel Avendano

Unable to move, staring in space,
you hear your heartbeat, too fast a pace.
It's 7 PM; what to do now?
Find peace of mind,
somewhere, somehow.

You find the strength to move off your seat,
head to the bathroom, shuffling your feet.
Look in the mirror, stare and stare...
you see the glass but your face isn't there.

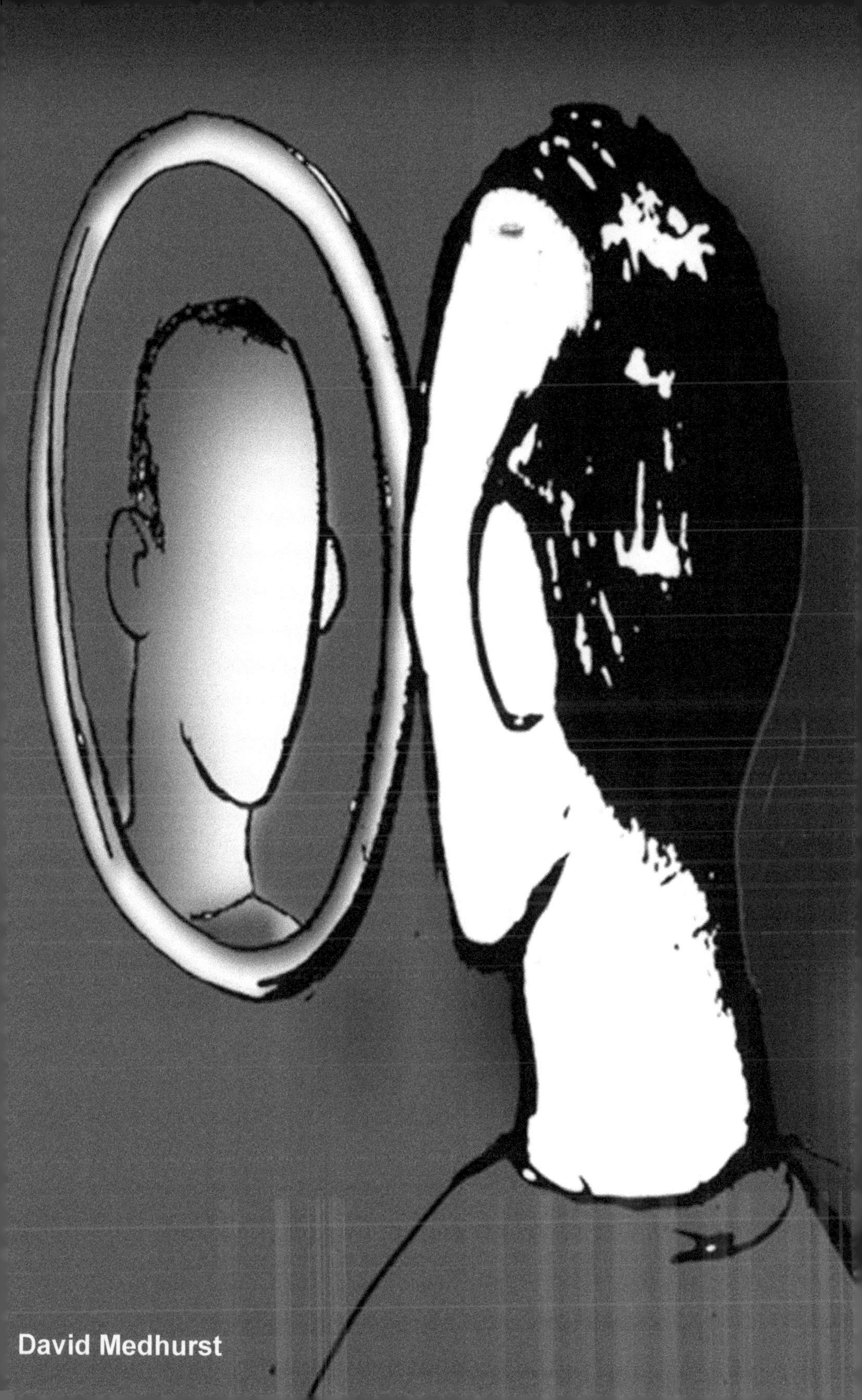
David Medhurst

Visibly older, bags under your eyes,
a picture of woe you cannot disguise.

Are you the one you've always been
or someone else you've never seen?

Take hold of yourself and wash away
these awful thoughts you've had all day.

Get undressed and go to bed,
relax your mind and clear your head.

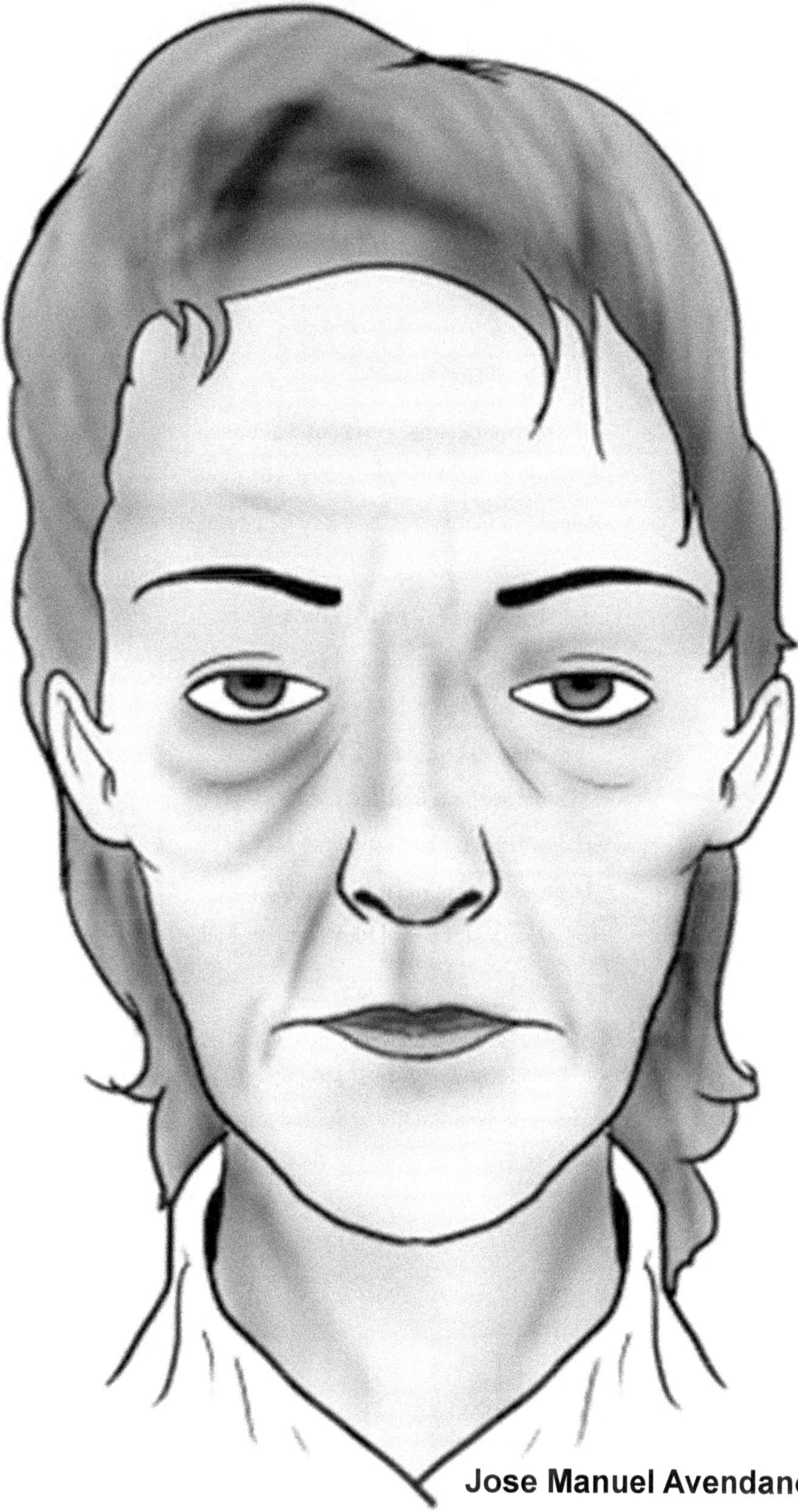

Jose Manuel Avendano

Under the covers, warm and secure,
nothing can bother you there, for sure.
You close your eyes and say a prayer:

Lord, I hope You're listening there,
for I feel so scared and full of fear.
I know I don't deserve Your ear,
because in the past I would insist,
there was no God; He didn't exist.
So, I'm turning to You as my last hope,
to give me strength to help me cope,
to help me sleep and wake refreshed,
feeling great, no longer depressed.

Thank you, Lord, for being so kind,
helping to ease my troubled mind.

David Medhurst

Waking up you look to see
that your clock is showing it's only 3.
Go back to sleep and snuggle in...
your 'TV show' will soon begin.

Closing your eyes the 'screen' is clear,
not long to wait, then you appear,
along with people you want to forget,
and situations that make you upset.

David Medhurst

It's a rerun, the scenes unfold,
making you sweat and your blood run cold.
The images of you, so obscene.
YOU HATE THAT PERSON ON THE SCREEN!

That person's not like normal folk,
WEAK AND USELESS, WHAT A JOKE!
Managed to hide it, now it's dawned,
on all these people...**THEY WERE CONNED!**

The foreman says, GUILTY at your trial,
you manage to escape but after a mile,
you fall and your clothes get ripped;
caught, now your dignity's stripped.

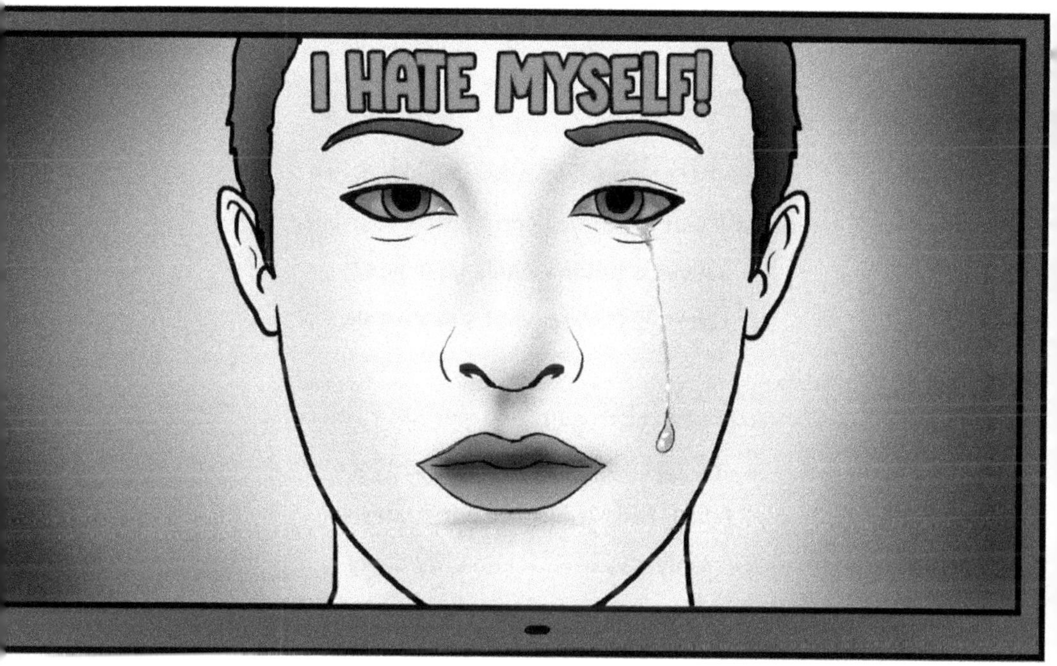

Jose Manuel Avendano

Just then you awake feeling like death,
in a state of panic, you can't catch your breath.
A voice talking inside your head.
Quiet! Listen to what's being said...

You've FAILED again, and you can't ignore,
it happened again like it did before.
A FAILURE today just can't survive.
Only a WINNER can stay alive!

Jose Manuel Avendano

You throw off the covers and leap to your feet,
put your head out the window, shout, then repeat...
'I can't take any more!' you yell to the sky,
'I can't take any more, this is HELL, let me DIE!!'

Jose Manuel Avendano

Part 2

The Concern

As morning comes the alarm starts to ring,
you're under the covers, so you won't hear a thing.
Who's that banging at your door?
You shout, "Go away!" but it starts once more.

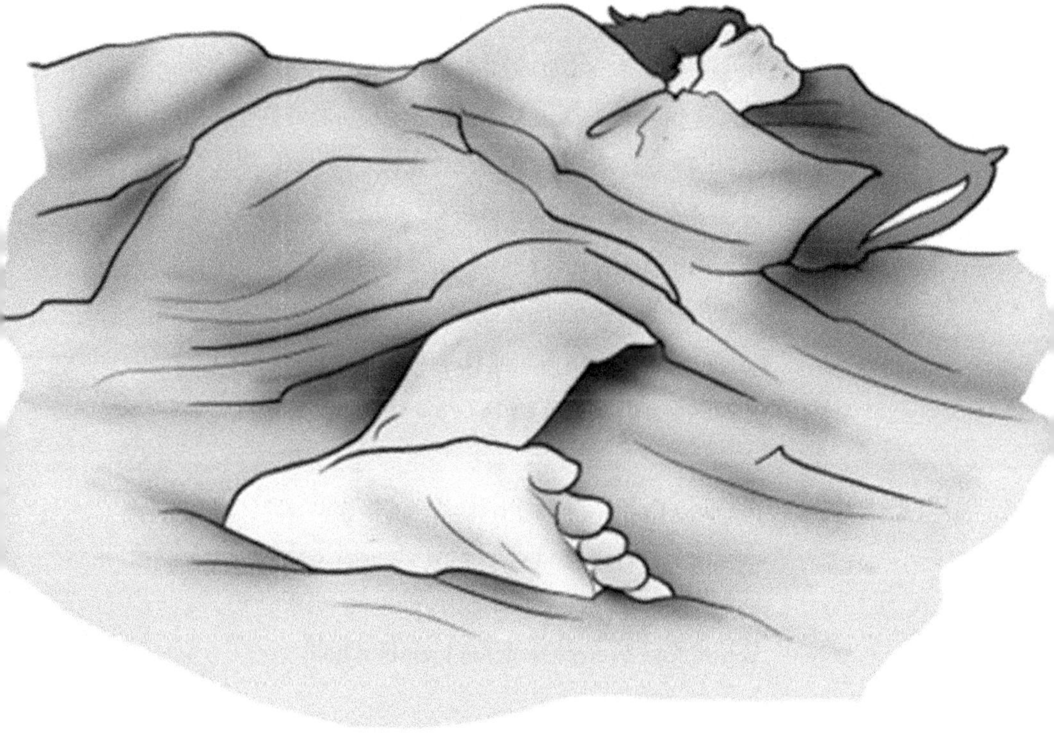

Jose Manuel Avendano

You get out of bed, forced from your haven,
unwashed for days and very unshaven.
It's so early; who could it be?
Through the peephole it shocks you to see...
your family and best friend there.
What do they want, as if you care?
How can you face them? Nowhere to hide.
They've heard you...need to bring them inside.

"You didn't answer when we tried to phone.
We were worried, and you being on your own...
we rushed down here, and it's just as well;
you've lost weight and you look like hell!"

Jose Manuel Avendano

Reluctantly you invite them in;
your place is one big garbage bin.
They ask you, "What on earth is wrong?".
But trying to explain it would take too long.

"You're just overworked", you hear Mum say.
"Pull yourself together, you'll be OK".
You have nothing at all to worry about,
so, come on now, stop acting out!"

It won't be long till they realise,
those 'things' you told them, weren't lies.
You are too depressed; things are out of hand.
It's not their fault...they just don't understand.

David Medhurst

Part 3

The Treatment

They make an appointment with your doctor.
What will she think when you go to talk to her?
Will she think you're mad and lock you away?
Locked up forever till you die one day?

But the Dr listens and she understands
when she sees your eyes and trembling hands.
"You need hospital treatment; take this letter.
You're very depressed; they'll help get you better".

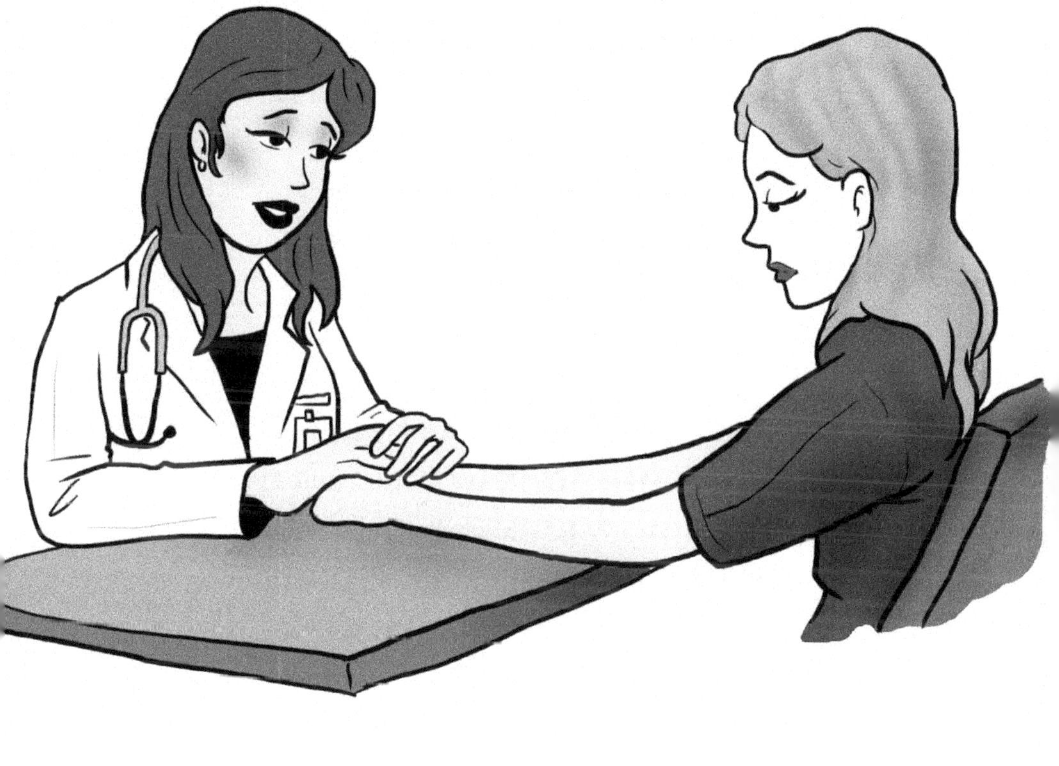

Jose Manuel Avendano

At the reception, they sign you in.
"Name, address, next of kin?"
"Fourth floor, sir, just follow the nurse".
Like going to my funeral, without the hearse.

You're shown to your room and left alone,
no problems, no bills, no work, no phone.
Then interviews start and never end,
driving you around the bend!

"My life is a mountain too hard to climb,
GET AWAY FROM ME, YOU'RE WASTING YOUR TIME!
I'm just a FAILURE, can't you see?
YOUR STUPID PILLS...THEY CAN'T HELP ME!!"

Staff try to convince you things aren't so bleak.
"Other patients here prove you aren't unique.
Although you can't accept it's true,
we've seen them get better, worse cases than you!"

Jose Manuel Avendano

Part 4

The Recovery

The first few weeks are hardest to bear,
unwilling to smile, unable to care.
"Hello!" says a patient in a friendly tone.
You point to your t shirt saying...
LEAVE ME ALONE!!

Slowly, but surely, the time passes by,
the pills start to work before you know why.
Used to be miserable, now instead...
the cloud of gloom drifts from your head.

Now your recovery's well underway,
mixing with patients, you've plenty to say.
Telling bad jokes and making them laugh...
THANK GOD FOR THE DOCTORS,
THANK GOD FOR THE STAFF!!

Jose Manuel Avendano

Who's that coming through the door?
Is it the one you used to deplore?
Full of confidence and self assured
LOOKS the same but now is CURED.

"Give away this bed, I'm over the worst,
to someone as ill as I was at first!"
You're a FAILURE no more, gone is the stress,
your new chapter's beginning... entitled SUCCESS!

Jose Manuel Avendano

It won't be long and you just can't wait,
to do all the things you used to hate.
Now your future can't be feared,
as words like FAILURE have disappeared.

You wake up early to enjoy the day,
and watch your gloom cloud fly away.
Feeling happiness you had thought gone forever,
living it, breathing it, a priceless treasure.

The time comes for you to leave,
knowing your experience has helped you believe,
that LIFE is precious and should be caressed,
WORTH LIVING FOR
when no longer DEPRESSED!

Jose Manuel Avendano

THAT'S FUNNY

Scary Hairy

Here is an example
from my observation hobby...
the balder the head,
the hairier the body!!

David Medhurst

Hot Flush

Sweating with relief,
having cured my constipation,
the toilet roll is empty...
cutting short my celebration!

David Medhurst

Right Formula

My boyfriend is a scientist;
our chemistry's just right.
We defy the laws of physics...
with biology each night!!

David Medhurst

Groan Deaf

Need hearing aids.
Specialist told me the price.
Couldn't hear him!

Dr. Erick Au.D

Feline Strange

My wife has so many cats
that last week one
of them bit her.
Now before she needs to 'go',
the toilet's filled with litter!

David Medhurst

Double Trouble

I've such a bad memory,
I committed the ultimate sin...
forgetting my sister's birthday,
when she happens to be my twin!!

Happy Birthday

Skirting the Issue

The kilted Scotsman
while playing golf,
had to make a decision whether...
to abandon his wayward drive
or be assaulted by the heather!!

David Medhurst

ROOTine Cheque

Sitting in the dentist's chair,
his laughter drilling through the air.
"A double extraction's
in store for you,
your tooth...and your savings too!!"

Jose Manuel Avendano

Urine Sample

"Urine sample, please".

I went before I got here.

I'm so peed off.

David Medhurst

Toupée Away

The bald man wears his
toupée with pride and dignity.
Try telling the wind!!

David Medhurst

SEASONAL

CHRISTMAS

Merry Blissmas

The big day draws near,
excitement, anticipation.
Not long 'til it's here,
the fun and vacation.

Owners light up their homes,
to compete for your admiration,
ignoring their hydro bills,
to join in the celebration.

The Christmas tree dressed,
tinsel, lights and more,
we're feeling very blessed,
as gifts surround the floor.

Christmas songs fill the air,
through speakers in each store,
Santa Claus in his chair,
kids line up by the score.

Praveen Singh Khati

But not everyone rejoices
or is so enchanted;
some don't have the choices
the rest of us take for granted.

Families split in half,
some left out at Christmas time.
No money, love or laughs,
that really is a crime.

Another **STUPID** Christmas,
just like in the past.
A 'give it a Missmas',
hope it goes by fast.

Praveen Singh Khati

What Christmas is about,
don't ever lose sight,
be sure to keep a look out,
for those you can invite.

To join you and your family,
as you celebrate,
all the Christmas fun and glee,
and the food that's on your plate.

Make each day a Christmas Day,
show its spirit in all you do,
and remember all those who pray,
for someone just like YOU!!

Praveen Singh Khati

NEW YEAR

Happy Now Year

A year has now ended,
a new one's just begun,
a year of ups and downs,
a year that's now done.

A year of some happy times,
a year of some sorrows,
a year of yesterdays,
todays and tomorrows.

A year of good health
and sickness for a few,
a year of lots of miracles,
out of the blue.

A year some family passed
and some close friends too.
A year babies were born
as life began anew.

A year of successes,
a year of mistakes,
a year you learnt a lot
and had some lucky breaks.

A year to pray
for all the wars to cease,
a year to be grateful,
for your freedom and for peace.

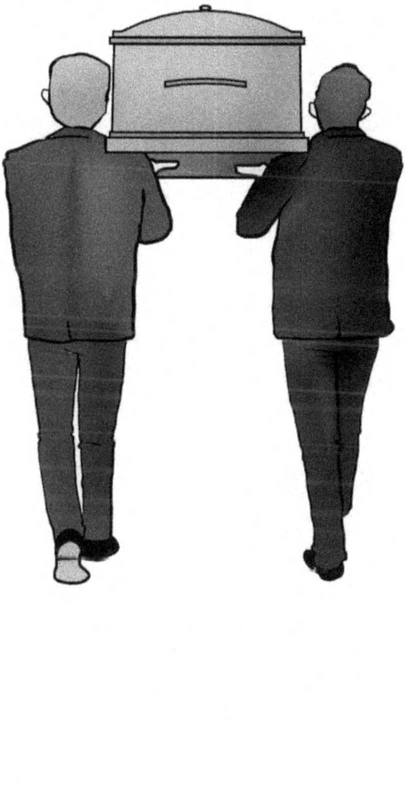

The illustration above is an exact copy of a photo of my late Mother feeding my twin sister Jackie and myself.

Make this a NOW Year to pause and reflect,
make this a NOW Year you'll never forget.

Make this a NOW Year to stick to resolutions,
make this a NOW Year to find the solutions.

Make this a NOW Year to stop complaining,
make this a NOW Year to get fit and start training.

Make this a NOW Year and make NOW what matters,
make this a NOW Year and leave your past in tatters.

Make this a NOW Year and believe you can do it,
make this a NOW Year to overcome and get through it.

Make this a NOW Year and make it WOW for YOU,
make this a NOW Year and your dreams will all come true.

Zoey is my cat.

Jose Manuel Avendano

Contact Alan Penn:-

e-mail
alanpennthepoet@gmail.com

Website: www.alanpenn.ca

Facebook
https://www.facebook.com/ThoughtsfromAlanPenn/

Instagram
https://www.instagram.com/thoughtsfromalanpenn/

Twitter
@FromAlanPenn

Linked In
https://www.linkedin.com/company/alanpenn/

Or send mail to:-
Alan Penn
Major Mackenzie Major Mackenzie Post Office
PO BOX 5085
Richmond Hill
Ontario
L4S 0B7
Canada

Lightning Source UK Ltd.
Milton Keynes UK
UKHW020654280521
384539UK00010B/524